Original title:
A House Made of Memories

Copyright © 2025 Creative Arts Management OÜ
All rights reserved.

Author: Miriam Kensington
ISBN HARDBACK: 978-1-80587-179-8
ISBN PAPERBACK: 978-1-80587-649-6

Dawn of Remembering

A creaky door, a morning yawn,
Cats parade across the lawn.
Pancake syrup, sticky hands,
Evidence of breakfast plans.

Old socks dance on the stair,
Giggling ghosts float in the air.
Grandma's hat with floppy rims,
Worn like heroes in our whims.

The Smell of Old Stories

Dusty books with tales so grand,
Whispers come from where they stand.
A chair that squeaks—what does it know?
Tales of laughter, high and low.

Mismatched cups, a teapot shy,
Sip the brew, watch time fly.
Cookies half-baked on the sill,
Sweet surprises bring a thrill.

Timeworn Treasures

Trinkets in a tangled mess,
Each one tells its own success.
A rubber duck, a tiny shoe,
Memories bubble, always new.

A clock that ticks but never tocks,
Counts the giggles, stacks of knocks.
Paintings crooked on the wall,
Smiles captured in each sprawl.

The Room Where We Grew

Crayon art on faded walls,
Adventure here, the best of calls.
Castles made from blankets wide,
Imagination's joyful ride.

A teddy bear, with button eyes,
Witness to our silly lies.
In this space of dreams and cheer,
Laughter lingers, always near.

Walls That Hold Secrets

In the corners, whispers lie,
Where my socks tend to sneak and hide.
Chasing shadows, I often sigh,
As the cat rules the world outside.

Pictures hanging, eyes that stare,
They giggle at my funny hair.
Every scratch tells a tale to share,
Of grand adventures unaware.

The Furniture of Time

My chair wobbles like a dance,
Potato chips had their chance.
With each creak, it joins the prance,
As memories spin, enhance.

The table's set for laughter's feast,
Where Sunday dinners never ceased.
A sticky note, my best beast,
Still holds the joke that's least released.

Shadows of Laughter

The shadows stretch, they play, they tease,
Like goofy ghosts with silly knees.
They dance through rooms, we share a breeze,
And leave us giggling with sweet ease.

Each bump and thud a punchline dropped,
With every blunder, joy has cropped.
In our abode, no jest is stopped,
The ceiling laughs, the floor just popped.

Windows to Yesterday

Through the panes, the world looks bright,
But bugs are drawn to porch light's bite.
They buzz and bumble, put up a fight,
While I swat wildly, quite the sight!

Reflections of friends lost in a grin,
Their silly pranks become my sin.
With every chuckle, we begin,
To cherish amidst this joyful din.

Where Time Stands Still

In the attic, we found old hats,
Big enough for rats and some stuffed cats.
Playing dress-up in the golden glow,
Time forgot us, and we loved it so.

Grandma's recipes, flour on our heads,
Trying to bake, but we burnt the breads.
Laughter echoed, smoke in the air,
Dinner was chaos, but who would care?

In the garden, we built a fort,
With wildflowers and a cardboard sport.
The neighbor's cat tried to join the fun,
We all took cover, but he was the one.

Evenings spent on the creaky floor,
Telling tall tales, who could ask for more?
Dad's snoring was the soundtrack we shared,
And the joy of this place, well, it was declared.

Sanctuary of Shared Dreams

We carved our initials high on the wall,
Later they faded, but we still recall.
A trampoline made from sheets and some chairs,
Bouncing through clouds without any cares.

Hide and seek beneath the kitchen light,
We'd giggle quietly, sneaking from sight.
Mom's slippers clattering, into the scene,
The look on her face was a comic routine.

With crayons and paper, we mapped out space,
Launching our dreams to an unknown place.
Aliens giggled from shadows nearby,
A crew of explorers, and we could fly!

At twilight, we'd share our fanciful tales,
Of pirates and mermaids, and faraway sails.
Though time might sweep us far from this zone,
In our hearts, this sanctuary is home.

The Colors of Connection

In the living room, we painted the walls,
Coloring chaos with splashes and brawls.
Purple polka dots and stripes of lime,
Who needs art classes when you've got time?

Chasing the dog with a sock on his tail,
We laughed so hard, we could hardly exhale.
He darted around like a furry brown blur,
Rolling in paint like it was a slur.

Sitting in circles, we sang off-key,
Uncles and cousins all joining with glee.
Though no one was perfect, every note rang,
The symphony played as our hearts sang.

And so we'll remember these moments so bold,
In a riot of colors, our love was retold.
Though life might take us on winding roads,
This laughter, this chaos, forever explodes.

Silhouettes of Happiness

In the attic, old toys lay,
Dusty bears in disarray.
A rubber chicken sits with pride,
As we laugh and reminisce wide.

The kitchen's filled with Auntie's stew,
Where mismatched socks have chatted too.
The fridge hums tunes of yesteryear,
While sticky notes gather cheer.

Jars of jellybeans in a row,
A sign of battles lost, you know.
Grandpa chuckles from his chair,
As we compete for nibbles rare.

Through the halls, we skip and slide,
On wooden floors, we take great pride.
Memories dance, a vibrant hue,
In this circus where dreams come true.

The Nostalgia Nook

Crusty books with tales untold,
Whiskers on the cat, so bold.
A clock that ticks but never sweeps,
In this nook, my laughter keeps.

Cushions plump, and tea gone cold,
Each sip has secrets to unfold.
The sofa's squeaks sing songs of joy,
Like giggles shared between a boy.

Chasing shadows in the glow,
Where silly hats and yodels flow.
An old piano, keys askew,
Echoes of mischief we once knew.

A thousand moments stitched so tight,
Wrapped in giggles through the night.
In this nook, we find our rhyme,
For memory's wink outlasts all time.

Memories in the Wallpaper

Patterns swirl like our delight,
A jungle gym in morning light.
Spilled juice stains dance and sing,
On the wall, our childhood fling.

Faded flowers by the door,
Whisper tales of games galore.
Here, a doodle, there, a heart,
Artful chaos, a true fine art.

Giggles echo off the seams,
Where fairy tales mix with dreams.
A tad of glue and some wild tape,
Creates a mishmash of escape.

From crayons bright to silly glee,
The walls hold us, a family tree.
In patterns old, our laughter stays,
Painting joy in subtle ways.

Stitched Together by Time

Knitted sweaters filled with cheer,
Each stitch a story, crystal clear.
The cat naps on a knitted square,
While yarn balls dance without a care.

Pillow forts like castles proud,
We sneak in giggles, loud and loud.
Blankets draped, our secret spot,
Where every moment means a lot.

A clock that ticks with knowing eyes,
Counts up the laughs and all the sighs.
Time's a friend in fuzzy socks,
As we sit and share our knocks.

With each sunset, laughter swells,
In stories told and ringing bells.
Through every quilt, our warmth aligns,
In this haven, love entwines.

Echoes of Stained Glass

Sunlight dances on the floor,
With shadows laughing at the door.
Grandma's plant still standing tall,
It knows my secrets, not a soul to call.

Cats knock over every vase,
Chasing dust bunnies in a race.
The curtains wave like they intend,
To spill the beans on every friend.

Silly hats from past birthdays hide,
Under the stairs, where memories bide.
Each trinket tells a silly tale,
Of pie fights and a dog named Gale.

Through every crack, the laughter sings,
Of moments wrapped with playful strings.
The echoes twirl in colors bright,
A kaleidoscope of pure delight.

Walls Whispering Stories

These walls have heard my loudest screams,
And yet they hold my softest dreams.
Every crack is an old embrace,
Filled with giggles from a familiar face.

Mismatched pictures on the wall,
Each frame tells tales of the fall.
Rainy days with puzzles spread,
And popcorn fights that left us dead.

Faded prints from little feet,
Trot through life on a comical beat.
The paint may peel, but love stays bright,
Each blunder wrapped in laughter's light.

Whispers float like leaves in air,
Telling secrets with giggles to spare.
These walls are snug, with tales untold,
Of cookie crumbs and friendships bold.

Foundations of Yesterday

Beneath the floor, the laughter lies,
With hidden treasures in disguise.
Old toys that once brought glee and fright,
Now gather dust when out of sight.

The creaky boards manage secrets well,
Of pizza parties and silly spells.
We danced too hard, the floorboards creaked,
In that moment, it was joy we sought and peaked.

Each scratch marks a story's trace,
With stickers stuck in a crooked place.
We left our fingerprints on the way,
Each footprint echoes, 'Let's love today!'

From forgotten dreams to playful fights,
These foundations hold our funny nights.
They barter giggles for the grace,
Of memories that time won't erase.

Treasures Beneath the Floorboards

Underneath where dust bunnies roam,
Lies the history we call home.
Old board games and mismatched socks,
Treasures hidden like magic rocks.

The vacuum cleaner's a monster, they say,
Eating up crumbs from our wild play.
Every thud is a stairway tale,
Of jump scares and pranks to unveil.

Make-believe kingdoms in the hall,
Where sheets transformed into castles tall.
With each step, a giggle pops,
As we reminisce over mishaps and flops.

Searching for candy, I found a shoe,
Wishing my grandmother's stories were true.
The whispers rise from each lost find,
A playful nudge from the past, unconfined.

The Spirit of the Space

In the corners, dust bunnies play,
They gossip about the chores of the day.
Fridge magnets hold secrets untold,
A collection of stories that never grow old.

The couch squeaks like an old man's laugh,
It tells tales of snacks, we'd bartered and half.
The clock ticks loudly, like a drum in the night,
Reminding us all we should turn off the light.

The echoes of laughter bounce off the walls,
While the cat plots revenge on the squeaky toy calls.
Each room a stage, where the family performs,
In a space filled with chaos where normalcy warms.

So here's to the quirks that make it feel right,
The odd little memories that spark pure delight.
As friends gather round for a night of great cheer,
We toast to the moments that we hold so dear.

Memory-Stained Floors

Oh the stains on the floor tell tales from the past,
Of spilled grape juice parties, oh what a blast!
From crayons to cookie crumbs under the chair,
Each mark is a memory, each spot has a flair.

There's a circle of pizza, left over from last,
That might just have been where the dog ate too fast.
Silly footprints dance from the door to the hall,
Each one telling stories, oh isn't that small?

The carpet's a map of the games that we've played,
Where hide-and-seek whispers and laughter were made.
Though the dust bunnies roam like they own the domain,
We cherish the chaos, in sunshine or rain.

So let's spill some more juice, let's leave some fresh prints,
For each little mishap is where love hints.
With every sad scrape or the coffee gone wild,
The floors know our hearts, they're perfectly styled.

An Ode to Windows

Oh windows, you keep all the laughter in,
You frame all the mishaps, the chaos, the grin.
You've seen every joke as we roll on the floor,
And the neighbors who think we are always a bore.

With smudged little fingerprints all over your glass,
You're a portal to worlds where the moments flash past.
You whisper our secrets to the sky up above,
While the curtains sway gently, just like our love.

Yet sometimes you tremble when tempests arise,
And we giggle at shadows that dance with surprise.
You capture the silliest scenes as they play,
Encoding our nonsense in bright sunray.

So here's to you windows, our view and our friend,
In your silly reflections, our laughter won't end.
You frame all our madness with charm and finesse,
Forever our portals to joy and success.

Mismatched Comfort

On this couch, half leather, half fluff from a dog,
We collapse into laughter, like the world's a big fog.
The chair with the stripes is a fashion faux pas,
Yet where else can I sit while I giggle and guffaw?

Grandma's old quilt, with patches of glee,
Wraps us in warmth like a hug from a bee.
The cushions are scattered, like thoughts gone astray,
Yet each little corner invites us to stay.

The lamp flickers rhythmically, keeping the beat,
As we dance on the carpet in brightly colored feet.
The mismatched socks are the stars of the night,
Making every round of charades a pure delight.

With laughter so loud and memories afloat,
In our odd little kingdom, we cheerfully gloat.
For comfort can't care if it's stylish or neat,
In our funny old nest, every quirk is a treat.

An Ode to Echoes and Shadows

In corners where laughter once danced,
Echoes of jokes still prance.
Shadows wear the past like a veil,
While cats chase dust, a comical tale.

Sticky notes cover the fridge like art,
Each one a memory, a quirky part.
The toaster hums tunes from days gone by,
As I ponder how time can really fly.

Transcending Dimensions of Home

A couch that swallows with open arms,
Pillow fights held by cushions' charms.
Socks go missing, a sock monster's thrill,
Who knew laundry could be such a skill?

Framed photos of relatives caught in a glance,
Always looking ready to start a dance.
Time travelers hanging, forever on hold,
Stories of laughter just waiting to be told.

Chipped Paint and Worn Carpets

Chipped paint tells tales of a wild ride,
Each scratch a secret, oh, how they hide!
The carpet's worn pattern, a maze of fate,
Hosting adventures, both silly and great.

The coffee stains join in on the fun,
Like badges of honor, one by one.
A dance party here? Oh yes, why not!
Just watch your step on that slippery spot!

Silent Songs of the Heart

In silence, the walls softly sing,
Of cheeky pranks and the joy they bring.
A fridge that hums a lullaby sweet,
Hiding leftovers, it's a culinary feat.

The bathroom mirror boasts of bad hair days,
Reflecting our highs, our awkward ways.
Each creak of the floorboards, a chuckle to share,
In this land of memories, we're a quirky pair.

Where Dreams Once Lived

In the attic, old shoes lie,
With mismatched laces, oh my, oh my!
They danced and twirled till the morning light,
Now they sit sore from their long, lost flight.

A chair that squeaks like a siren's song,
Once held my dreams, where I'd belong.
Now it wobbles, a tad too weak,
But it's got stories that still can speak.

The sofa's springs, they have their say,
When you sink in, they squeak 'Hooray!'
It holds my snacks and midnight chats,
Oh how it loves our little spats!

Where laughter echoes, memories thrive,
In this quirky maze, we come alive.
With every corner, a tale unfolds,
In this wonderland of stories told.

Photographs in the Dust

A snapshot taken on a sunlit day,
Grandpa caught mid-dance, in disarray.
His shoes untied, his hat askew,
The wall now creaks, but it still holds true.

Dust dances gently on the frame,
Each smile and fumble, never the same.
A family picnic with too much cake,
You'd think great grandma would learn her mistake!

The cat in the corner, a royal boast,
With crumbs on its fur, it loves to coast.
Each picture tells tales of laughter and cheer,
Even that time mom spilled soda in here.

Photographs whisper of days gone by,
The silly moments that made us cry.
With every click, a piece of our heart,
Captured forever, never to part.

The Heartbeat of Home

The fridge hums a jolly tune,
While socks sneaked off to an early noon.
Coffee spills on a Tuesday morn,
Because chaos is where love is born!

The floor creaks under tiny feet,
As giggles echo, oh what a treat!
A dog in the corner, dreaming away,
Chasing squirrels on a sunlit day.

The walls hold tears, some laced with glee,
Stories unfold, as wild as can be.
Each crayon mark, a mural of fun,
In this heartbeat, we soar and run.

When doorbells ring, we leap and dash,
Caught in the whirlwind of love's sweet smash.
In this embrace, we're tangled and tight,
Ah, the real magic of pure delight.

A Tapestry of Remembrance

Threads of laughter, stitched with care,
Quirky moments, beyond compare.
Grandma's quilt with patches of cheer,
Every square holds a tale so dear.

One patch a dance in the rain that day,
Another's a trip where we lost our way.
With mismatched socks, we played our part,
In this tapestry that warms the heart.

Stains from dinners that went astray,
Burnt toast adventures, oh what a play!
Each meal a journey, an epic quest,
In this fabric of life, we find our rest.

Laces tangled, stories we weave,
In every corner, we find reprieve.
This tapestry hugs us, holding us tight,
With every thread, we spark pure delight.

Crayon Scribbles on the Floor

Crayon colors on the wall,
A masterpiece, or a call?
Mom's a painter, Dad's a sage,
Age is just a scribbly page.

Cats sit proud, their tails a swirl,
While chaos dances, twirls and twirls.
Sneaky snacks beneath the chair,
Who needs a diet? Who would care!

The fridge hums in a friendly tone,
Telling secrets of its own.
Dance-offs happen, socks in the air,
While dad's secrets are found everywhere.

So let the colors run until late,
These tiny scribbles are simply great.
Forever young in a wibbly line,
Royalty with each crayon sign.

A Whisper in the Breeze

Leaves rustle softly like a friend,
Whispers of secrets that never end.
The wind laughs gently, pulling your hair,
With memories dancing without a care.

Silly hats and runaway kites,
Chasing giggles on sunny nights.
In a garden where dreams can grow,
Petunias and daisies put on a show.

A dog barks tunes that could spell 'fun',
As butterflies flutter under the sun.
Each gentle breeze recounts a tale,
Of ice cream drips and a bicycle trail.

So listen close next time you sigh,
For laughter and joy are floating by.
In a world where the wind has its say,
Nothing is serious; it's still child's play!

Echoing Footfalls

Tiny feet patter like rain,
A game of chase, and then again.
Giggles reverberate off the wall,
As shadows chase, and memories sprawl.

A treasure hunt beneath the bed,
Forgotten friends that never fled.
Marbles rolling, the clock strikes three,
Racing cars and a loud 'Whee!'

Hallways echo with a playful shout,
Can never find what we're about.
An old shoe becomes a space rocket,
Exploring planets from every pocket.

So let the footfalls dance and sing,
From kitchen combat to lively spring.
In every step, a story to tell,
In this happy chaos, we dwell.

Daydreams in the Den

Cushions piled to reach the stars,
As we zoom on imaginary cars.
Laughter erupts from a comfy nook,
Where every look is a brand new book.

Pajamas on a Sunday morn,
In our world, nothing can be worn.
Build a fort from what we find,
With milk mustaches and dreams combined.

Shadows creep like secret spies,
While midnight snacks, oh, what a prize!
A movie marathon with no one to judge,
And popcorn wars, we'll never budge.

Daydreams whisk us far away,
In our den where we forever play.
So gather round, let's share a grin,
For every heartbeat, there's joy within.

Roofs of the Unforgotten

Under the tiles where laughter flew,
Cats, and dogs, they all just knew.
Spilled milk fights, a slippery floor,
Ice cream wars, oh, who could ask for more?

Socks tossed high, they danced in glee,
A game of tag with grandma's tea.
Jokes exchanged with each sunrise,
Who knew that food could cause such sighs?

Pictures hung, but one's askew,
Is that dad? Or uncle Lou?
Grandma's cookies in the air,
Sneaking bites, without a care.

Memories stacked, like dusty books,
Finding treasures, just take a look.
Under the roof where all was bright,
They still giggle in the moonlight.

Cracked Foundations of Joy

Creaking floors that sing of cheer,
Every crack holds a joke so dear.
Jumping high, an epic flop,
Laughter echoing, never stop.

The cellar's dark, a monster's lair,
But with a flashlight, we don't despair.
Bouncing balls in every nook,
A hide-and-seek, the best storybook.

Squeaky hinges tell of fights,
Over the last dance on summer nights.
The fridge hums tunes from a distant land,
Where all the best snacks are simply planned.

The porch swing whispers to the breeze,
Old rocking chairs that aim to please.
In cracks of joy where laughter grows,
A time capsule, how time just flows.

The Scent of Familiarity

Cinnamon mornings with burnt toast flair,
That odd sock found under the chair.
Dad's old cologne mixed with play-doh,
Laughing at things we just let go.

The aroma of chaos, sweet, yet odd,
Grandma shouting, "I love a good prod!"
Sticky fingers from candy runs,
Shh… quieter, here come the puns!

Familiar scents that tug at heart,
Like old movies, a classic art.
Every whiff a tale unfolds,
In this space, laughter never grows old.

The smell of mischief baked in pies,
Where laughter lifts and never dies.
In essence, joy sticks in the air,
Among these scents, joy is the faire.

Rooms Filled with Stories

Walls that echo the tales untold,
Of vanishing socks and children bold.
The living room, a drama show,
With pillows flying, and friends in tow.

The bathroom's where the songs are sung,
Rubber duckies and bells were rung.
With splashes loud and voices high,
Comedic acts that catch the eye.

Closets lined with fears and dreams,
That come alive in giggling schemes.
Every corner, a pirate's delight,
Sailing through blankets on stormy nights.

The attic holds treasures so absurd,
Like hats for cats or a funny bird.
In every room, a jest or thrill,
Laughter lurks, and time stands still.

Ribbons of Life Twisted in Beams

In the attic, old things lay,
A frog-shaped lamp that lost its way.
With each step, the floorboards creak,
They chuckle back, so to speak.

That vase with flowers from '88,
Its colors scream, a vibrant fate.
Grandma's scarf, a tangled mess,
Fashion faux pas, we must confess.

A cat once hid beneath the bed,
Sprang out when Auntie Moore's face turned red.
Dust bunnies dance in swirling loops,
Recalling parties with laughing troops.

So many stories wrapped in threads,
Every corner, laughter spreads.
In this room, the joys collide,
Ribbons tangled, love and pride.

The Doorway to Yesterday's Light

Upon the door, a squeaky tune,
Echoes of laughter, morning's rune.
A sock lost in the coat rack's grip,
Adventures gone on a wild trip.

Fridge magnets spell our messy dreams,
Pickles in jars, or so it seems.
An oven mitt with a cartoon grin,
Bakes the memories, thick and thin.

We'd dress up as pirates in a quest,
Grandpa's hat, we thought it best.
Time-traveling in pajamas, bold,
With a magic remote, tales retold.

This doorway whispers, tales await,
Past giggles linger, it's never too late.
To step inside what once was bright,
And dance again in yesterday's light.

Lanterns of a Time once Bright

In the yard, old lanterns sway,
Flickering back to yesterday.
Each glow a giggle, a candy dare,
In corners where secrets dared to share.

A hula hoop spins with a laugh,
Counting each trip, impossible math.
The trampoline springs, a flight of glee,
Who knew we'd bounce back so carefree?

Red and green lights across the porch,
Twinkling laughter, we never scorched.
Children running with ice cream dreams,
Dripped on shirts, or so it seems.

Time's lantern flickers, rumors spread,
Every shadow a story, lightly read.
With whimsy bright, we shine the night,
Lanterns dance, our hearts take flight.

The Rooms that Hold Our Secrets

In the closet, where old coats sigh,
A treasure trove of the reasons why.
The polka-dot dress that once caused glee,
Now an artifact of youthful spree.

Drawers filled with cards and notes,
Stories tucked with secret quotes.
The living room, where grandpa falls,
Telling jokes 'til laughter stalls.

A cookie jar that holds the past,
Empty now, but memories last.
Under the couch, an old lost shoe,
Whose was it? We'll never construe.

Each room whispers tales of yore,
With echoes dancing on every floor.
Secrets linger in each cracked beam,
As we laugh and share the fading dream.

An Embrace in the Shadows

In the corner sits an old cat,
Wearing my socks as a hat.
Laughter echoes through the halls,
Where wallpaper peels and the paint balls.

A chair that rocks and creaks with glee,
Telling tales of cups of tea.
The ghosts of toast burned a bit,
In a kitchen where the spatula's split.

Memories dance like shadows at dusk,
With ticklish secrets and unshaken trust.
Grandpa's jokes make the floorboards creak,
While grandma's recipe brings a cheeky peek.

Every nook holds a grin or a frown,
As we stumble in our wedding gown.
What a ride, this quirky shindig,
In this space, we're all big kids!

The Cradle of Remembering

A cradle swings but takes a snooze,
With toys that sing out silly blues.
A teddy bear with a crooked smile,
Laughs at every strange denial.

The fridge is full of leftover pie,
With one poor slice just wondering why.
In the attic, a bicycle lies,
Dusty dreams under the skies.

Photos hang at odd angles, tight,
Where Uncle Joe wore his shoes too bright.
Ticker-tape memories swirl and noodle,
As we dance in circles, quite a poodle.

In our hearts, the giggles don't stray,
They bop and weave in a funny ballet.
Each echo a memory that rocks,
In our silly, cherished paradox!

Portraits of the Past

Old portraits hang with grumpy grins,
As if they know all of our sins.
A family tree with a crooked trunk,
Where the fruit of laughter's never sunk.

The dog that barks at the mailman fun,
Plays tag with shadows—oh, what a run!
Old shoes with laces all untied,
Telling stories of silly pride.

Every shelf holds a crazy fight,
Over puzzles that weren't just right.
Bid the dust a laughing goodbye,
As the past winks back from the sky.

Silly spoons dance at half-past four,
As memories bubble from the floor.
We're all portraits in a sunny frame,
With laughter's echo, ever the same!

Voices in the Quiet

Wisdom whispers through the air,
With echoes of my grandma's stare.
Socks mismatched in a laundry spree,
Cheeky reminders of calamity!

The clock ticks loud with a sarcastic grin,
Counting moments like a comic win.
A rubber chicken says hello,
As we relive every goofy show.

The fridge hums a familiar tune,
Baking cookies by the light of the moon.
In this quiet, there's a jig and a jive,
With every heartbeat, we come alive!

Voices chuckle, drift and sway,
As we gather round at the end of the day.
In the calm, our laughter is loud,
In this silly, loving, cherished crowd!

Mementos in the Attic

Up in the attic, what do I see?
A rubber chicken, winking at me.
Old hats and boots, a puppet parade,
And a gift from grandma that always decayed.

Dusty old boxes with secrets inside,
A disco ball shining, oh what a ride!
Grandpa's old records spin tales of yore,
While Auntie's sock collection just makes me snore.

A quilt full of patches, a story or two,
Of my dog with a wig, looking fierce and askew.
Pictures of family, all laughing with glee,
Remind me that life's just a grand comedy.

So here in the attic, I giggle and grin,
Amidst silly treasures, this treasure trove's win.
With every odd item, a chuckle, a cheer,
For the past is a circus, and I'm the ringmaster here!

Threads of Yesterday

Spools of laughter, threads of delight,
Colorful fabric that dances in light.
Grandma's old apron, a patchwork of dreams,
Hiding odd stories, or so it seems.

Stitching together the joy and the tears,
Every thread whispers, 'Let go of your fears.'
A sock with a hole from the dog's little bite,
Only adds charm to my childhood plight.

Ribbons are tangled, and buttons are loose,
Yet through every knot, there's a giggle or moose.
My teddy in tatters still gives me a wink,
What would he say if he learned how to think?

So here I stand, tangled but free,
With threads of yesterday, all dancing with glee.
Each patch tells a tale, a funny mishap,
In this colorful chaos, I take a quick nap!

Conversations with the Walls

The walls whisper tales when the night is still,
Of shoes on the roof and a cat with a will.
They giggle at moments, both silly and sweet,
Like the time my dad tripped over his own feet.

The wallpaper peels with a mischievous grin,
While ghosts of old echoes invite me to spin.
I chat with the curtains, they sway and they fluff,
Saying, 'Remember that time? You thought you were tough!'

In corners they chuckle at secrets they hold,
Of midnight snacks and stories retold.
Each crack in the plaster, a laugh shared in time,
While the windowpane watches, a friend in a rhyme.

So here I sit, listening with glee,
As the walls share their laughter, just they and me.
In this home of mischief, where memories play,
Every conversation just brightens my day!

Faded Paint and New Beginnings

The walls are a canvas of history's brush,
With smudges of laughter and a bit of a rush.
On faded horizons, the colors compete,
Like my brother's old bike lying there at my feet.

Cracks in the plaster bear witness to fun,
A paint splatter fight that was quickly undone.
'New colors for growth?' I muse on the thought,
But the chaos and quirks are the gems that I've sought.

Each drip of the paint tells a story untold,
Of birthday surprises and sibling jokes bold.
Spray cans are waiting, new dreams on the rise,
While the chipped yellow corners just giggle and sigh.

So here I embrace every color and crack,
For with faded old memories, I never look back.
In this lively abode, where quirks intertwine,
Faded paint and new dreams all brightly align!

The Dance of Dust Motes

In sunbeams bright, they take their flight,
Little twirls and tiny leaps,
Caught in laughter, lost in light,
Waltzing on the air, in heaps.

With a giggle, one takes a dive,
A pirouette, a bump, a glide,
They shimmy through, they come alive,
In this dusty ballroom, they hide.

A sneeze erupts, they scatter wide,
Off they go, like butterflies,
Through rafters high, the memories ride,
Whispers sweet, like old goodbyes.

When cleaning time begins its drill,
The dance breaks out, a wild spree,
As dusters fly — oh, what a thrill!
A party that sets spirits free!

A Library of Laughter

Books with faces, oh what a sight,
They chuckle and snicker with glee,
Pages flipping, a grand delight,
Spilling secrets, wild and free.

There's a tale of a cat that sings,
And one where shoes have a ball,
Dancing mice on paper wings,
A library where giggles call.

Pen and ink, a playful plot,
Every character full of cheer,
With every plot twist, laughter's caught,
In a nook, cozy, never austere.

So grab a book, let joy invade,
Lose yourself in dreamy lore,
In this library, fun's never delayed,
Read, laugh, and come back for more!

Balconies of Belonging

Up high they stand, in sun and shade,
Flower pots and bright swings,
Chairs creak with tales we made,
And laughter's tune softly rings.

Neighbors pop in, with cookies to share,
Each silly story we unwrap,
Helium balloons float in the air,
Our balcony, a laughter map.

The wind tells jokes, makes us sway,
Chasing clouds, we laugh out loud,
As sunsets paint the sky that day,
In our corner, we feel so proud.

So raise a glass, hear the cheer,
On these balconies, joy is free,
Together in laughter, we persevere,
In every story, you and me!

The Diary of Our Days

Oh dear diary, what a mess,
Spills of milk, and socks in pairs,
Stories tangled in childhood dress,
Laughter echoes, filled with dares.

Every mishap, big and small,
Is scribbled here with silly flair,
With doodles that just rise and fall,
A montage of whimsy, beyond compare.

We danced in rain, we lost a shoe,
Whipped cream fights and silly hats,
Each page holds laughter, tried and true,
In this book of joy, not just spats.

So flip the pages, let's relive,
These cherished days that gleam and glow,
In our hearts, we learn to forgive,
Turning moments into a show!

Memory's Silent Portraits

In dusty frames, the laughter stays,
Where gramps wore socks in silly ways.
A birthday hat upon a cat,
The dog, it seems, was quite a brat.

With every glance, a chuckle's found,
The artist's flair, a tiny hound.
A garden gnome with painted eyes,
Is now our chief in grand disguise.

Each corner holds a wobbly chair,
Where secrets whispered, floating air.
A wig from Uncle Joe appears,
He wore it once, and brought us cheers.

The rug's a canvas of our past,
With spills and stains, our lives amassed.
A place for socks and secret snacks,
Mountains of laundry, little hacks.

A Symphony of Footsteps

Each morning brings a marching band,
With slippers sliding, oh so grand.
The cat, a maestro, leads the spree,
While dad conducts with coffee, glee.

From kitchen crescendos to living room,
Where socks perform in perfect gloom.
The squeaky floors, their own refrain,
A waltz with crumbs at my domain.

The echo of our joyous strife,
The plop of food, the dance of life.
Grandma's tap shoes, worn and bright,
Join in the fun, day or night.

And when the sun begins to set,
The sounds of laughter linger yet.
A symphony of slams and squeaks,
Our daily tune, a love that speaks.

Light through the Cracked Pane

Sunbeams giggle through the flaws,
In window frames with laughter's cause.
Each crack reveals a tale or two,
Of ghosts that played peek-a-boo.

The dust motes dance, a lively crew,
While shadows lounge in coffee blue.
A sunbeam's warmth, a silly prank,
We wave goodbye to the little bank.

The potted plant, a witness loyal,
To every little ruckus, royal.
With leaves alive, they seem to cheer,
As mum spills tea and grunts, oh dear!

The light plays tricks, it hides, it seeks,
Creating spots for jumping freaks.
And in those rays, our laughs encase,
The silliness we can't erase.

The Staircase of Past Adventures

Stairs known for shouts and tumble plays,
Where socks have vanished, gone for days.
Each step a story, up and down,
Of ancient trips and mom's lost crown.

The railing's grip, a leaping guide,
With echoes from the chaos wide.
The ghost of jam that once did spill,
Is now a legend, sweet and ill.

Memories carved in splintered wood,
Of wild races, no one thought they could.
A skateboard ride, a daring feat,
The neighbor's yard became our street.

And on each landing, tales unfold,
Of treasure hunts and secrets bold.
These steps may creak, but so do we,
In the dance of life, so wild and free.

Shadows of Laughter and Tears

In corners where socks lose their pair,
Laughter echoes, a sweet love affair.
The cat sits, plotting a stealthy attack,
While we chase our memories, never look back.

Spilled juice on the floor, a dancefloor so grand,
Footprints of chaos, a toddler's command.
Silly faces in photos, oh what a sight!
Capsized adventures on a wild starry night.

When walls start to whisper their funny tales,
Of thunderous giggles and curious gales.
Each shadow, a friend in this wild escapade,
With every chuckle, our silly charade.

And in this mayhem, peace does reside,
A refuge of warmth, where we laugh and abide.
So let the jokes roll like the dishwasher's tune,
Here's a toast to the crazy, beneath the full moon.

Windows Framed in Remembrance

Through windows adorned with smudged little hands,
We laugh at the chaos that no one understands.
Once a pancake breakfast turned into a war,
This kitchen's a battle—who's cleaning the floor?

The dog barks at nothing, he owns the backyard,
Chasing his tail like a comedic bard.
Each ding in the wall tells a story so sweet,
Of whims and of wishes, and runaway feet.

Oh, those sunlit memories, a light-hearted dance,
Playing Monopoly turned quite a chance.
With fake money flying, and laughter so loud,
We became legends for the family crowd.

From each pane of glass, our past takes a peek,
Reacting with silliness, hardly unique.
Here's to the stories we hold in our hearts,
In windows of laughter, where friendship starts.

The Roof that Held Our Dreams

The roof above creaks with stories untold,
Of pillow fights raging, and laughter so bold.
Slippers on wood floors, a soft symphony,
Each step tells a tale, oh such harmony!

The attic's a treasure with hats long gone,
Played dress-up today, but tomorrow at dawn.
With old photo albums, we're time travelers still,
Replaying our moments, with hearts we fulfill.

Each rain on the shingles becomes a soft tune,
Melodies of mischief sung under the moon.
We built our dreams here, on laughter's great beams,
Under the roof, we soared higher than dreams.

And as shadows play in a kooky ballet,
Our hearts stay forever, in this grand array.
So here's to the roof, our whimsical frame,
In this silly abode, we've made our own name.

Timeless Corners of Comfort

In the corner that holds the old tattered chair,
Stories are whispered, with dust in the air.
Silly debates on who's the best cook,
And sneaking some snacks like a mischievous crook.

The cushions absorb all our giggles and sighs,
With eye rolls and chuckles, our love never dies.
Tickling the baby till she squeals with delight,
The hours melt softly, like day turns to night.

In timeless embrace, these corners remain,
Where hearts feel at home, through joy and through pain.
We'll gather together, no matter the weather,
With stories or blanket forts, we're light as a feather.

And though the world outside sometimes seems tough,
In our cozy enclave, we've got all the stuff.
So let's raise a toast in the warm, sunlit glow,
To the comfy corners where we're free to grow.

Envelopes of Emotion

In the drawer, old cards reside,
Each with a tale, a grin, or a slide.
One says, 'Remember that awful cake?'
I laughed so hard, I almost did break.

Dusty photos stacked in piles,
Each snapshot brings forth endless smiles.
The dog in a hat, looking so grand,
Now that's a treasure, quite unplanned.

Letters from friends, some quite absurd,
Of all the things said, the funny word.
Like socks on a penguin, or pies in the sky,
These silly moments make time fly.

Memories dance like shadows at dusk,
Wrapping us tight in a warm, fuzzy husk.
Each envelope bursts with laughter and cheer,
A testament of joy for all who come near.

Fragments of the Familiar

The chair that squeaks with every sit,
Echoes of laughter that just won't quit.
From spills and thrills to snacks we share,
Each fragment funny, with stories to spare.

The kitchen's alive with chatter and clinks,
Spaghetti fights and too much drink.
A plate is tossed, my dance is quite grand,
My moves, like pasta, slip right from hand.

Random socks stuffed in the couch's seam,
They've become a part of our daily dream.
The dog sniffs them out, what a dizzy find,
In this maze of nonsense, peace of mind.

A half-full cup of questionable tea,
Grown cold with stories, just like me.
These fragments of us, so quirky and real,
Color our lives with a warm, funny feel.

An Inventory of Intimacy

A rubber duck with a cracked old grin,
Swims through memories of laughter within.
It squeaks a tune of our joyful past,
In this wacky inventory, we hold fast.

Forgotten board games stacked, oh so high,
With rules that change each time we try.
"Skip me, it's your turn!" is the common refrain,
In this joyous chaos, we always gain.

Old t-shirts, stained with time's little stains,
Tell tales of dance-offs, from whence it gains.
We wear them with pride, mismatched and bold,
Our history, woven, never grows old.

The curio cabinet's filled with oddities galore,
Dust bunnies whisper, "Please give us more!"
With each quirky piece, laughter takes flight,
In this inventory, our hearts feel so light.

Musings in the Front Porch

Rocking chairs sway to a tune of the past,
Each squeak tells secrets, memories cast.
A cookie jar with a smiley face,
Holds relics of snacks in a cozy embrace.

Sunshine spills over the faded wood,
As we share stories, both silly and good.
Like the time the cat stole my ice cream cone,
And ran with it fierce, such bravery shown.

Neighbors wander by with a wink and a sigh,
As we reminisce, with laughter nearby.
I swear that lawn gnome chuckles with glee,
In our front porch realm, it's just you and me.

With mugs in hand and the world at our feet,
We muse about life, what a quirky treat!
In this simple space, joy feels alive,
Our memories bubble, forever they thrive.

Doors to Forgotten Moments

There's a door that squeaks just right,
Every time I creep at night.
It creaks out tales of dog and cat,
And how we fought for the last spat.

In the attic, a hat shaped like cheese,
Made us giggle and brought us to knees.
With memories stuck on each dusty box,
We laughed so hard till we lost our socks.

Behind the wall, a faint sound drips,
Not echos of words, just snacktime trips.
A ghostly hiccup, a drippy sigh,
And stampede of kids who'd fly by.

Beneath this roof, mischief reigns bright,
Silly faces in the soft moonlight.
Each moment a dance, a twirl, a spin,
Even the cat joins—let the fun begin!

The Garden of Lost Time

In a garden where weeds like to plot,
We once planted dreams, but forgot the lot.
With flowers that giggle when tickled by air,
They bloom out stories beyond compare.

A gnome with a grin, so large on his face,
He whispers secrets of this funny place.
Rabbits wear glasses, quite fancy indeed,
Reading our fortunes while munching on seed.

Butterflies gossip while sipping on dew,
Wishing they'd flown with the picnic crew.
Spilling the snacks, we'd laugh till we cried,
As ants marched in line, feeling dignified.

In this quirky patch, there's not much rhyme,
But weeds hold laughter of a lost time.
So let's plant some joy, make a cluttered scene,
In this garden of giggles, silly yet keen!

Chasing the Ghosts of Us

There's a shadow that dances on days gone by,
With a wiggle and giggle, it says hi!
We chased it down streets paved in schtick,
Swapping our socks for a comical trick.

The echoes of laughter bounce off the walls,
Reminding us of our silly brawls.
We raced for the cookies, a cunning heist,
Our sweet tooth smiles, quite uninvited, spiced.

In the twilight, we'd whisper our dreams,
With hot cocoa spilled, or so it seems.
A ghostly grin and a wink to share,
Chasing those moments as light as air.

With each haunting giggle, the past comes to play,
With knock-knock jokes that never decay.
Forever we roam in this laughter-filled quest,
Chasing our shadows, we feel so blessed!

Candlelight and Comfort

In the glow of candles, we gather round,
Telling tall tales where laughter is found.
With waxy drips and a fresh-baked loaf,
Our stories unfold like a warm, fuzzy cloth.

Flickering light dances on faces so bright,
S'mores in hand, oh what a delight!
Marshmallows toasted, they stick to our cheeks,
As we share all our joys, our giggles, our tweaks.

A blanket of warmth wraps us tight,
With shadows like friends bobbing in sight.
The clock clicks away, while we jest and play,
Candlelight hugs us, urging us to stay.

So here's to the moments we made without fuss,
In a flicker of candlelight, it's all about us.
With giggles and marshmallows, our hearts feel light,
In this cozy embrace, everything's just right!

Recollections in the Shadows

In corners where odd socks reside,
We chuckle at spills we can't abide.
The cat sits proud, with a toothy grin,
As if to say, 'Let the chaos begin!'

With echoes of laughter that fill the air,
We find frayed edges everywhere.
The clock ticks slow, a comic parade,
Of all the fun plans that we never made.

We wave at the dust bunnies on the floor,
Reminding us of the lives we bore.
Each creak in the floor, a tale to tell,
Of mishaps that turned out just swell.

In shadows of rooms, the memories cling,
Where each tiny blunder feels like a king.
We shrug off the mess with a hearty cheer,
For laughter, you see, is what's truly dear.

The Lantern of Reminiscence

There's a lantern hanging crookedly low,
Illuminating all our highs and lows.
With firefly jars that never stay closed,
We giggle at stories that time has imposed.

The chairs are mismatched; it looks like a show,
As friends crack jokes and steal the dough.
Cookies burnt black are deemed a fine art,
While we decorate cakes with wild, crazy hearts.

Old photos in frames are a riot of glee,
With hairstyles that scream, 'What was that spree?'
We reminisce over outfits absurd,
Each memory a line, in laughter, confirmed.

In this light of nostalgia, we gather and smile,
Turning mishaps to gold with each chuckled mile.
So raise up your glass, let's toast to the fun,
For in every disaster, our spirits are spun.

Beyond the Threshold of Time

Past the threshold where the dust bunnies roam,
Lies a world crafted from laughter, our home.
With mismatched shoes lined up by the door,
We wonder who wears them, now and before.

Whiskers twitch at the tales on the wall,
Of romps through the garden, we had a ball.
Shoelaces tangled in a dog's daring chase,
Each moment a treasure, a laugh on our face.

Socks that went missing come back with a flare,
Dancing in corner posts with a bold, wild air.
We grin at the memories that flicker like light,
With each playful stumble, we're feeling just right.

In this quirky abode, time's games are so sly,
Turning frowns to grins, oh, my, oh, my!
With every new chapter, we gather to rhyme,
For our lives are a symphony, beyond the sands of time.

The Knitting of Souls

In a cluttered nook where the yarn balls roll,
We weave funny tales, heart and soul.
Knitted together by stitches and puns,
We laugh till we cry—it's how we have fun.

Hooks clicking loudly, the cat gives a leap,
A yarn ball disaster, our secrets to keep.
With colors so bright, patterns out of hand,
Our friendship is threaded, though crazy and grand.

With needles and wit, we stitch life's design,
A patchwork of moments, both silly and fine.
Tangled in laughter, our stories entwined,
Each loop a reminder of the joy we find.

So let's raise our mugs, a toast we will make,
To the loom of our lives, and what we create.
For though we get jumbled in life's wild sprawl,
Together, we conquer, each stumble, each fall.

An Archive of Echoes

A creaky floor, a rumble of boots,
Old socks dancing, in mismatched pursuits.
The cat in the corner, with a sarcastic glare,
Judges our parties, like it just doesn't care.

Each photo a story, with wigs made of foam,
This wild wild life, we celebrate home.
Grandma in disco, spitting out tea,
In a polka-dot dress, oh how can it be?

Ice cream for breakfast, or was it a dream?
With laughter so loud, bursting at the seams.
Spilled beans on the carpet, what a grand feat,
Our slip-and-slide games are on repeat!

Memory echoes, they tickle and tease,
Tales told to old chairs that sigh in the breeze.
We laugh at the chaos, all silly and bright,
It's the echoes of love that dance in the light.

Hearthstone Reflections

Flames flicker and giggle, a marshmallow fight,
Uncle Timmy's burnt toast is a terrible sight.
We giggle and munch, with crumbs on our face,
As gravity loses its grip in this place.

The clock on the mantel can't keep up the pace,
Time's running wild in this spunky old space.
Each calendar page, a parade of odd days,
Where socks turned to superheroes in hilarious ways.

With stories of quirks, we sit by the fire,
Imagining astronauts in a rubber tire.
Giggles erupt like popcorn in a pan,
As the cookie jar sneaks away with the pan!

Shadows move gently, like whispers of glee,
As we poke and we prod at our old family tree.
A family so joyful, so jumbled and real,
With quirky reflections wrapped in every meal.

Fading Footsteps

Footsteps echo, a tap dance of old,
With mismatched shoes and a story retold.
A wig in the closet, a pirate's old hat,
Ballet on the kitchen floor, imagine that!

The curtains are bowing, with secretive flair,
As a dust bunny rolls by, shows he doesn't care.
Strange shadows perform on the walls with wild grace,
While laughter finds corners, in this silly space.

A treasure map leads to a cookie tin prize,
While squirrels plot schemes with mischievous eyes.
The dog thinks he's captain, with his tail in a whirl,
As the soup pot plays music and starts to twirl.

We dance among memories, fading yet bright,
In a scrapbook of chuckles, our hearts feel the light.
Each footstep a giggle, a cute little blip,
A merry-go-round of our love's funny trip.

The Attic of Longing

Up in the attic, where time takes a leap,
With old toys and dreams buried far, far deep.
A hat on a mannequin, waving hello,
While the ghosts of our laughter nudge us to grow.

With a trunk full of secrets, all tangled with grace,
Where the past plays hide-and-seek, cheeky in space.
A rubber chicken sings, in its own silly tune,
As the dust motes pirouette like little balloons.

We find forgotten costumes, mismatched and bold,
As the attic's board creaks, with stories untold.
The flashlight beams laughter, upon all old things,
Echoing joy in the attic, where sunlight still sings.

So we dance through the clutter, with giggles that soar,
With whispers of yesterdays knocking at the door.
Each box holds a treasure, of joy and of cheer,
In this attic of longing, where memories are dear.

Carvings in the Woodwork

Look at that scratch made by the cat,
Framed like a masterpiece, imagine that!
The chairs creak like old men in a chat,
Hauntingly funny, where's the ghostly spat?

Stains from juice spills tell tales of their own,
A rainbow of chaos, lovingly sown.
Each mark on the table, a laugh we have known,
Our grand life's a show and we're overthrown.

The doorbell rings like a trumpet so loud,
Scaring the mailman, oh what a crowd!
The woodwork chuckles, it's drawing a crowd,
In this funny old place, we laugh like we're proud.

With memories plastered, what stories reside?
Our quirky adventures can't be denied!
So grab a spot, let's let our hearts glide,
In our rustic abode, there's nowhere to hide.

The Quilt of Our Existence

Stitched together by threads of old laughs,
Each fabric a tale, recounting our gaffes.
Got a patch for the dog who chewed on our drafts,
Memories sewn with love, our home's epitaphs.

A corner for mishaps, a square for old gripes,
From mishandled dinners to odd acolytes.
Every crease and fold sparks joy like bright pipes,
A quilt made for snickers, not just for swipes.

The colors are bright like a clown's big shoe,
Every thread holds a giggle, a mishap or two.
Sometimes the humor is like a wild zoo,
Wrapped in our blanket, we chortle anew.

When shadows grow long, it's cuddles we chase,
Draped under laughter, the silly embrace.
Your foot in my face, but I'll never erase,
The quilt of existence, our favorite place.

Whispers of the Past

The clock ticks loudly, mocking our fears,
In shadows it chuckles, through all of the years.
It's seen all the blunders, collected our tears,
A witness to giggles, and outlandish cheers.

Ghosts of our pranks echo deep in the room,
They float past the windows, dressed up in gloom.
With voices like whispers that dance through the gloom,
Reminding us gently, we're never consumed.

There's a mischievous spirit, quite fond of our snacks,
Who guffaws at our troubles and eats through our packs.
With poltergeist breadcrumbs, it keeps us on track,
Our home's a mad circus, with laughter, not hacks.

So lift up your glass to the whims and the giggles,
To whispers that jiggle and joyful wiggles.
The past may be tricky, like a wild sneeze wiggle,
Yet here we are laughing, our joy's not a wriggle.

Echoes in the Hallway

Down the long hallway, echoes bounce back,
    Footsteps tell stories as I lose track.
A dance with the vacuum? Oh, what a knack!
Each squeak and each creak, I'll keep 'em on tap.

The walls are adorned with mismatched frames,
    Photos of faces and silly games.
I swear that one picture still calls me names,
With winks and shenanigans, it fuels our flames.

When I call for the cat, a ghostly reply,
Seems memories linger, like a chicken that flies.
They giggle and whisper with mischievous sighs,
    Echoes of laughter that never quite die.

So stroll through the hallway, let humor unfold,
    Embrace the old tales that never grow cold.
For a life filled with laughter is better than gold,
    The echoes of joy are a treasure to hold.

Faded Photographs on the Mantel

Old snaps of grandpa, with hair like a mop,
Curly mustaches that never would stop.
A dance with a cat, in mismatched shoes,
What a sight, oh who could refuse!

A birthday party, ice cream in the air,
Uncle Fred face-planted, we gasped in despair.
Mom's bright smile captured, and dad's goofy pose,
Tickling our memories, how time quickly goes.

The Christmas that ended with pudding cat fights,
But laughter stuck with us, like dazzling lights.
So here on the mantel, these joys sit to stay,
Our lives wedged in frames, like a favorite play.

With faces that wink and stories that tease,
These faded old photos put hearts at ease.
For in every capture, a giggle resides,
A life full of glee, with our memories as guides.

Where Time Softly Knocks

In the hallway whispers, time slips and slides,
A clock that can't keep up with its tides.
Tickle fights echoed through the kitchen so wide,
Where grandma's old cookies would never abide.

A vase full of laughter, a teapot of cheer,
Mom's secret recipe, lost, but we're near.
Cooking disasters, flour flew like a dream,
The neighbors all giggled, or so it would seem.

Each room holds a chuckle, a dance, just for fun,
The wall paints our stories, with secrets to run.
When time softly knocks, it brings with it glee,
A heartbeat of laughter, forever set free.

In corners and edges, where sunlight peeks through,
Frolicking memories weave stories anew.
So let's raise a toast, to each giggle and quake,
To the home that we built, with each memory we make.

The Attic of Forgotten Hopes

Dusty old treasures that dance in the air,
A bike with one wheel and a feathered chair.
We climb up the ladder, in search of the fun,
To find all our treasures, in rays of the sun.

Boxes of trinkets from long ago times,
A ukulele, a globe, a can full of limes.
Old letters from cousins, each one is a joke,
We laugh till we tumble, all under the cloak.

A snow globe that sings of a snowy delight,
But it's lost all its magic, and now it just bites.
Tangled up ribbons and posters all torn,
Just like their memories, they laugh as they mourn.

In our attic of hopes, we chuckle and cheer,
For the past isn't faded, it's shimmering here.
With each silly memory, the hopes we once had,
Get dusted and glittered, making us glad.

Hearthstone Reflections

The fire's warm glow, like a friendly old friend,
Where stories are shared, and giggles transcend.
Marshmallows burn sweet, kids racing about,
While dad's telling tales that are full of a sprout.

The shadows are dancing, doing the twist,
As cats chase their tails, in a comical mist.
Flames crackle with laughter, the night's full of cheer,
Each flicker a memory, like popcorn, they appear.

A comfy old chair and a blanket or two,
Where grandpa would snore, but we bet he flew.
With goofy expressions, and socks on the floor,
These hearthstone reflections beg us to explore.

In each glowing ember, there's a giggle anew,
A story retold, with a humorous view.
So gather round close, share a laugh or two,
For laughter by firelight, is the best thing to do.

Charmed Corners

In the kitchen, pots all clatter,
Grandma's recipes that used to splatter.
Sauce on ceilings, cookies in hair,
Laughter echoes, joy everywhere.

Couches sagging from all our weight,
Oops, spilled juice—oh, what a fate!
Cats on the table, dogs in the chairs,
Charmed corners filled with fun and cares.

Every shadow holds a tale,
Dancing socks with a jolly fail.
Tickles and hugs in the hallway twist,
Mom says, 'Stop! I can't resist!'

Sunshine beaming through every nook,
Jars of pickles and the funny book.
Together we roam, our spirits high,
In these corners our dreams fly.

The Legacy of Light

Sunshine dances on the floor,
Tripping over toys, I swore!
Caught in the chase, my foot slips loud,
The clock strikes joy in the jumbled crowd.

Dust bunnies roam and take their stance,
Under the couch, they like to prance.
Brushing off cobwebs from the light,
Each flicker tells a joke, pure delight.

Silly shadows jump on the wall,
Grandpa's stories that make us sprawl.
With every laugh, the warmth ignites,
In this glow, we craft our sights.

Candles burning at the dinner table,
Every flicker tells a tale, if you're able.
In these moments, we gather bright,
Building our legacy of light.

Beneath the Surface

Under the bed, old treasures lie,
Mismatched socks, oh my, oh my!
Lost action figures, a rogue toy car,
Squeaky clean? Not by far!

Beneath the rug, a mystery grows,
Crayons, crumbs, and a pet that glows.
Who needs a vacuum? We've got fun,
Messy games till the day is done.

Tunnels of pillows, fortresses grand,
Where epic battles of laughter stand.
Monsters lurk 'neath every chair,
Not a worry, just giggles in the air.

Underneath it all, a giggling mess,
Each little secret, we would confess.
In the chaos, we find our way,
Joy hides beneath—come out and play!

Handprints on the Wall

Crayon scribbles in a rainbow spree,
Colors of joy—look, there's me!
Handprints scattered, a painter's delight,
Every page turns into a sight.

Sticky fingers on the fridge,
Oops! A splash over the edge.
Mama laughing, not in a rage,
Artistry born from a playful stage.

Windows streaked with finger trails,
Stories woven where laughter prevails.
Each mark a memory, loud and clear,
Whispers of warmth from those we hold dear.

Each corner painted with love's sweet call,
Woven in laughter, we've built it all.
Handprints cherished, the scribbles tall,
In this gallery, joy stands tall.

Chasing Ghosts through Hallways

In the hallway, shadows play,
I swear I heard my socks say,
They've been hiding, what a ruse,
Left me searching for my shoes!

Nights are filled with whispered cheer,
A light flickers, then disappears,
What's that sound? A ghostly snort?
Or just my cat in a report?

Laughter echoes, walls do shake,
Every creak, a funny break,
An old chair squeals; what a scene!
Was it my snack—or a meme?

In each corner, memories roam,
Old jokes finding their way home,
While I swipe at dust with glee,
Who knew ghosts could laugh with me?

Garden of Echoed Joy

In the garden, blooms may sway,
But so do jokes I hear each day,
A pot's caught laughter with such flair,
It's hard to tell if plants can care!

Tangled vines, a bright bouquet,
Sprouting giggles in the May,
A sunflower takes up the mic,
Singing tunes both funny and hype!

Caught in laughter, bees do buzz,
They're crafting honey, just because,
The daisies dance in silly rows,
Even weeds have punchlines that glow!

With each bloom, a memory grows,
Mirthful whispers in the throes,
Nature's humor fully caught,
In this plot, I've found a lot!

The Dust of Heartfelt Reminisce

Dust motes float on sunbeams' play,
Stirring up tales from yesterday,
An old sock fights a battle grand,
With a dust bunny's fluffy hand!

On the shelf, a trophy gleams,
For best pillow fight in dreams,
Every scratch marks joyful fights,
With laughter echoing through nights!

Old chairs creak with secret stories,
Of couch potato glories,
Beneath my bed, the past does cling,
With lost things wearing their old bling!

Dust collects and holds a smile,
Reminding me of every trial,
As I sneeze with a chuckle nice,
Each memory—a framed slice!

Dreams Tacked to the Walls

On the walls, my dreams hang tight,
Like post-it notes in morning light,
One says, 'Dance like no one's here,'
The other reads, 'Dinner's over, dear!'

Memories stick with tape and cheer,
A calendar clowning through the year,
Big laughs pinned in crayon hues,
Spaghetti sauce on my best shoes!

Each corner sports a silly face,
That giggles back from its safe place,
A framed diploma, huge and bright,
For champion of pillow fights!

With every glance, I'm met with glee,
As dreams remind me, 'Just be free!'
These tacked-up thoughts make life a ball,
In this cozy home, love conquers all!

www.ingramcontent.com/pod-product-compliance
Lightning Source LLC
Chambersburg PA
CBHW070004300426
43661CB00141B/213